Ayudantes de la comunidad / Helping the Community

¿Qué hacen LOS BIBLIOTECARIOS?
What Do LIBRARIANS Do?

Mary Austen
Traducido por Eida de la Vega

PowerKiDS
press

New York

Published in 2016 by The Rosen Publishing Group, Inc.
29 East 21st Street, New York, NY 10010

First Edition

Editor: Katie Kawa
Book Design: Katelyn Heinle
Spanish Translator: Eida de la Vega

Photo Credits: Cover (librarian), pp. 1, 13 Mark Edward Atkinson/Blend Images/Getty Images; cover (hands) bymandesigns/Shutterstock.com; back cover Zffoto/Shutterstock.com; p. 5 SharonPhoto/Shutterstock.com; p. 6 Sergey Novikov/Shutterstock.com; p. 9 © iStockphoto.com/MattoMatteo; p. 10 Tyler Olson/ Shutterstock.com; pp. 14, 24 (computer) © iStockphoto.com/3bugsmom; p. 17 © iStockphoto.com/ JasonDoiy; pp. 18, 24 (library card) SW Productions/Photodisc/Getty Images; p. 21 Brenda Carson/ Shutterstock.com; p. 22 wavebreakmedia/Shutterstock.com; p. 24 (computer) Hywit Dimyadi/Shutterstock.com.

Library of Congress Cataloging-in-Publication Data

Austen, Mary.
What do librarians do? = ¿Qué hacen los bibliotecarios? / by Mary Austen.
p. cm. — (Helping the community = Ayudantes de la comunidad)
Parallel title: Ayudantes de la comunidad.
In English and Spanish.
Includes index.
ISBN 978-1-4994-0647-4 (library binding)
1. Librarians — Juvenile literature. 2. Libraries — Juvenile literature. I. Austen, Mary. II. Title.
Z682.A97 2016
020'.92—d23

Manufactured in the United States of America

CPSIA Compliance Information: Batch #WS15PK: For Further Information contact Rosen Publishing, New York, New York at 1-800-237-9932

CONTENIDO

CONTENTS

Una biblioteca es un lugar
con muchos libros.

A library is a place with
many books.

Puedes pedir prestados libros
de la biblioteca.

You can borrow books
from the library.

También puedes pedir prestadas películas y música.

You can borrow movies and music from the library, too.

Un bibliotecario es alguien que trabaja en la biblioteca.

A librarian is someone who works at a library.

Los bibliotecarios te ayudan a buscar libros. También te ayudan a buscar música y películas.

Librarians help you find books. They also help you find movies and music.

En las bibliotecas hay **computadoras** que la gente puede usar. Los bibliotecarios te pueden ayudar a usar las computadoras.

Libraries have **computers** for people to use. Librarians can help you use the computers.

Los bibliotecarios también
te ayudan para que puedas
sacar cosas prestadas de
la biblioteca.

Librarians also help you borrow
things from the library.

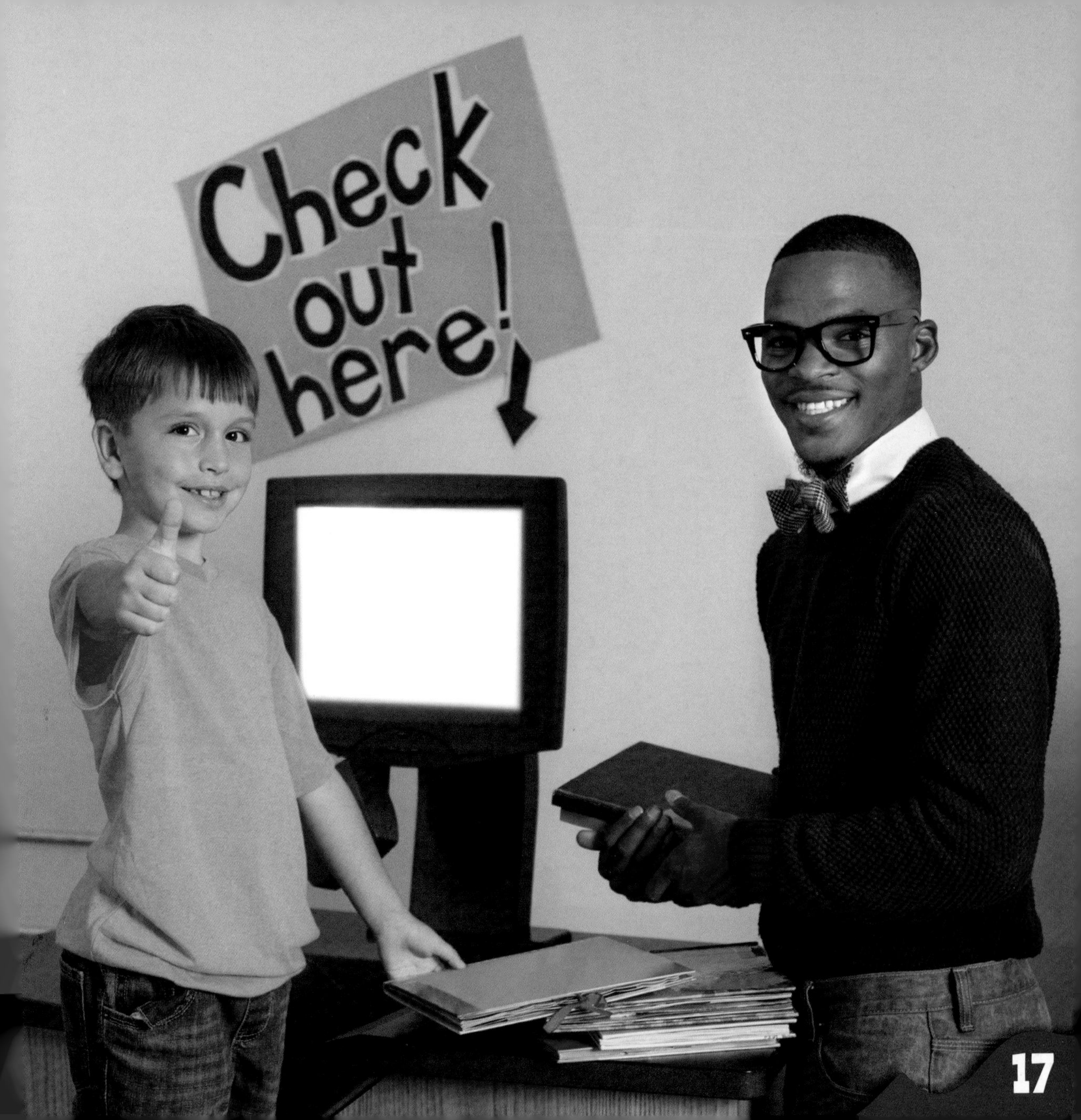
Check out here!

Primero le muestras al bibliotecario tu **carné de biblioteca**. Entonces, ya puedes sacar cosas prestadas.

First, you give the librarian your **library card**. Then, you can borrow things.

En la biblioteca puedes hacer actividades. ¡Puedes hacer manualidades!

You can also do activities at the library. You can make crafts there!

Los bibliotecarios hacen
que la biblioteca sea
un lugar divertido.

Librarians help make the
library a fun place to visit!

PALABRAS QUE DEBES APRENDER
WORDS TO KNOW

(la) computadora
computer

(el) carné de biblioteca
library card

ÍNDICE / INDEX

SITIOS DE INTERNET / WEBSITES

Due to the changing nature of Internet links, PowerKids Press has developed an online list of websites related to the subject of this book. This site is updated regularly. Please use this link to access the list: www.powerkidslinks.com/htc/lib